I0528656

Brian
The Therapy Quail

by

Beth Koenig

In Memory of
Brian the Quail
2017 - 2022

Special thanks to Johnny Lam, without whom Brian and this book would not exist.

Brian the Therapy Quail © Copyright 2023 Beth Koenig

All rights reserved. No part of this publication may be reproduced, distributed or transmitted in any form or by any means, including photocopying, recording, or other electronic or mechanical methods, without the prior written permission of the publisher, except in the case of brief quotations embodied in critical reviews and certain other noncommercial uses permitted by copyright law.

Neither the author nor the publisher can be held responsible for the use of the information provided within this book. Please always consult a trained professional before making any decision regarding treatment of yourself or others.

For more information, email info@therapyquail.org

ISBN:
978-1-961965-00-3 (soft cover print)
978-1-961965-01-0 (ebook)
978-1-961965-02-7 (audio book)

Meet Brian

Brian is a therapy quail. He helps people feel better. He helps them keep calm and be happier. He is a good bird!

1

Brian started out as an egg. He was in a special box called an incubator to keep him warm.

After 18 days, Brian was ready to come out of his egg! He hatched!

At first, learning to walk and flap was hard. But Brian and his siblings kept trying.

They learned where their food
and water were kept, too!
Soon they were able to play
chase with each other.

Brian was a good companion from an early age. He enjoyed standing on a hand and looking around while chirping.

Brian also loved being held! He happily looked around while being carried and enjoyed all the attention he received.

Brian's favorite part of bathtime is drying off. He shakes his feathers, and the water flies around him!

Brian loves going for walks and exploring the backyard. He never knows what he might find. Maybe a tasty snack!

One of Brian's favorite activities is crowing. He crows to let his friends know where he is and to tell others to be nice.

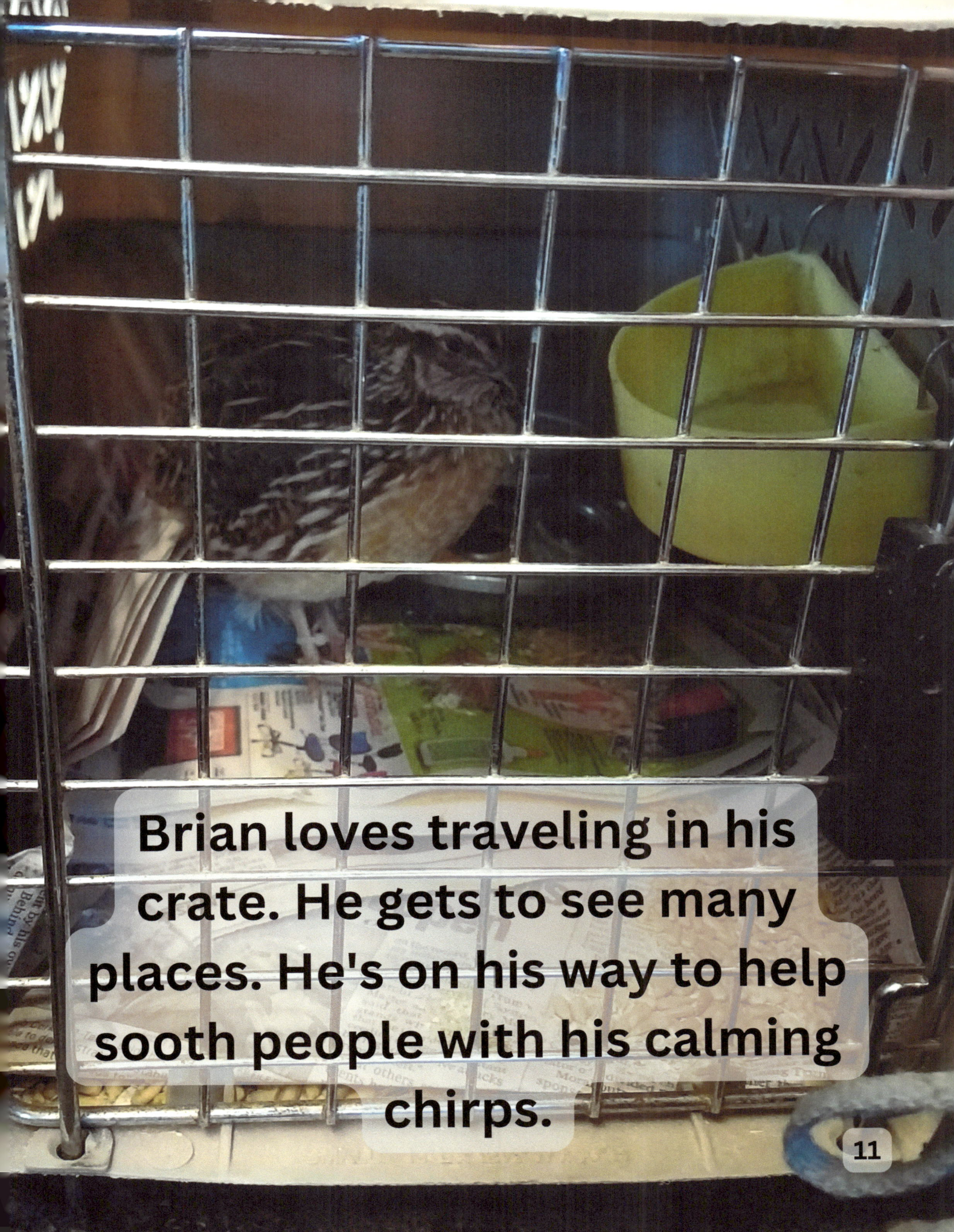

Brian loves traveling in his crate. He gets to see many places. He's on his way to help sooth people with his calming chirps.

Brian has even gone on airplanes. He loves looking out the window and seeing what it is like to fly!

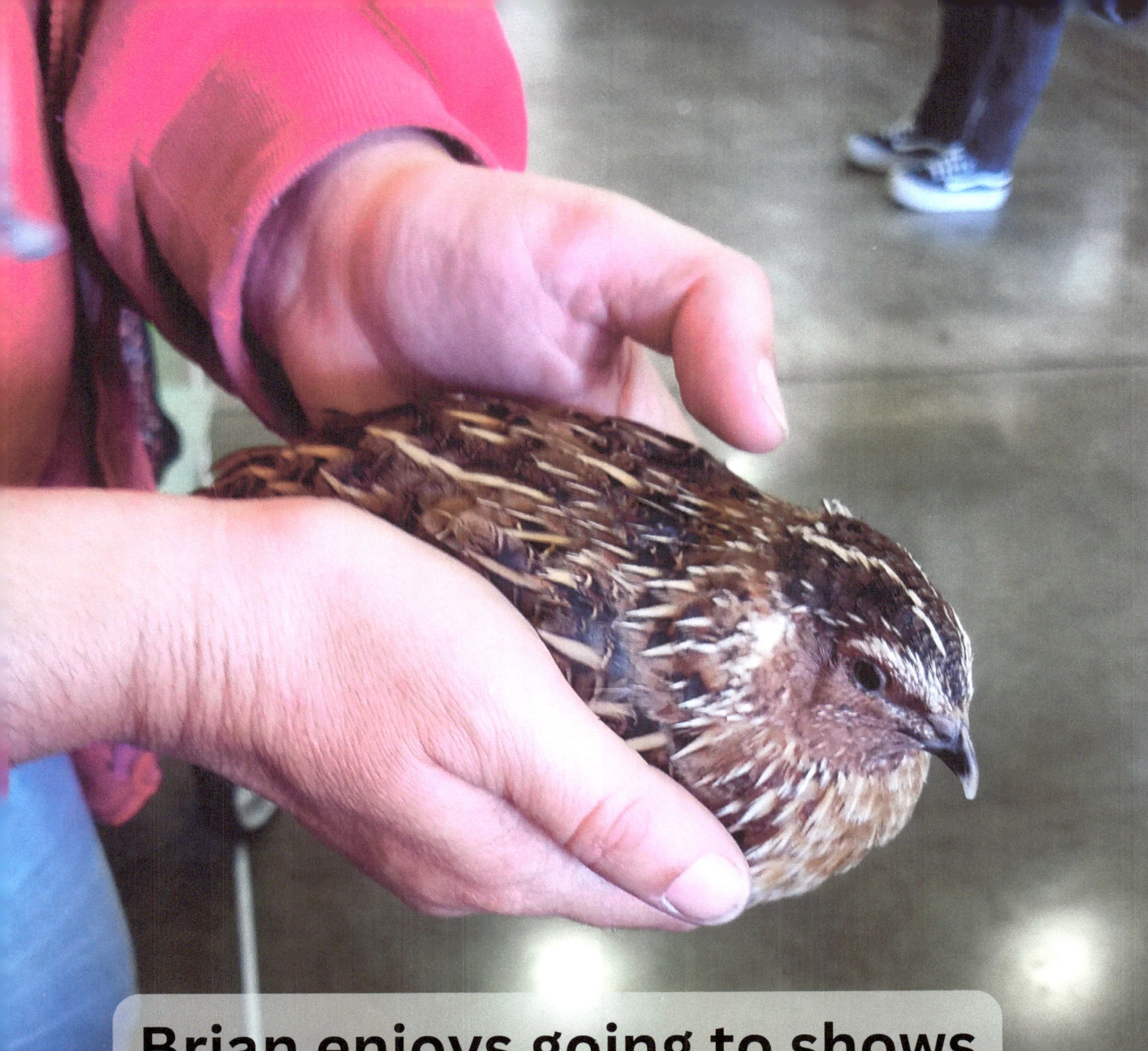

Brian enjoys going to shows where people stop to pet him and ask questions. He loves teaching people about quails!

When Brian is done working, he likes to come home and rest with his friends.

Brian loves to take a nap after a long day and dream about tomorrow's adventure.

Facts About

- Japanese coturnix quail like Brian can live up to 6 years.
- Quail are easy to care for.
- Quail do best either by themselves or in a cage with one male and two females.
- Therapy quails are domesticated birds that have been socialized to be therapy animals.
- Quail are easy to handle and transport because they are smaller than most other therapy animals.
- Quails are social animals that enjoy interacting with humans.

Therapy Quail

- Quails make an excellent therapy animal because of their calming and soothing presence.
- Japanese coturnix quails are low-maintenance birds that require only basic housing and nutrition.
- Quails make a soothing sound when they chirp, which can help create a relaxing environment.
- Therapy quails can be used to treat autism, anxiety, post-traumatic stress disorder (PTSD), and a variety of other conditions as a form of complementary therapy.

Learn More About Brian and Other Quails

Therapy Quail

therapyquail.org/activities

Sign Up for:

Videos
Activities
Coloring Pages
and More!

www.ingramcontent.com/pod-product-compliance
Lightning Source LLC
Chambersburg PA
CBHW041452120626
46547CB00002B/426